FINANCIAL PLA

A GUIDE TO ACHIEVE YOUR PERSONAL FREEDOM BY
BUILDING A STRATEGIC MONEY PLAN FOR YOUR LIFE

Descrierea CIP a Bibliotecii Naționale a României

   Financial Planning. A Guide To Achieve Your Personal Freedom By Building A Strategic Money Plan For Your Life. – Bucharest: My Ebook Publishing House, 2018
   ISBN 978-606-983-624-8

FINANCIAL PLANNING

A GUIDE TO ACHIEVE YOUR PERSONAL FREEDOM BY BUILDING A STRATEGIC MONEY PLAN FOR YOUR LIFE

My Ebook Publishing House
Bucharest, 2018

CONTENTS

INTRODUCTION

*I want to use this means to thank and congratulate you for downloading this book "**Financial Planning: A Guide To Achieve Your Personal Freedom By Building A Strategic Money Plan For Your Life**"*

We should start by making a critical refinement. "Plan," is both a verb and a noun. We see effortlessly that the verb, or the activity of planning, precedes the thing, or the "plan." Put differently; the plan is the yield of the planning process. In this way, financial planning is an activity or series of moves made with the aim of producing an extensive financial plan. Contained inside the plan are more moves to be made, yet these activities are not "financial planning," as such, yet somewhat activities identified with your financial life, for example, saving and contributing.

When we have a financial plan, we would then be able to start to make a move on the procedures and strategies laid out in the plan that push us toward accomplishing our coveted objectives in life. Hence, the financial plan turns into a dynamic, all-encompassing guide, redid to the individual (couple, or family), from which more move is made, as fundamental, to advance us through the essential occasions in our lives.

Thanks again for downloading this book and I hope you enjoy it.

CHAPTER ONE

FINANCIAL PLAN, A CONTEXT FOR BUSINESS

A financial plan is an extensive review of an investor's present and future financial state by utilizing promptly known factors to foresee future cash flows, resource values, and withdrawal plans. Most people work in conjunction with a financial planner and use current total assets, charge liabilities, resource allotment, and future retirement and domain plans in creating financial plans. These metrics are exploited alongside appraisals of benefit development to decide whether a man's financial objectives can be met later on, or what steps should be taken to guarantee that they are.

This verity frequently incorporates spending which sorts out a person's accounts and now and then includes a progression of steps or particular objectives for expenditures and sparing later on. This plan assigns future wage to different sorts of costs, for example, lease or utilities, and furthermore holds some pay for here and now and long-haul funds.

Financial plans don't have a particular layout. However, most authorized experts incorporate learning and contemplations of the customer's future life objectives, prospect resources exchange plans, and potential cost levels. Extrapolated resource values decide if the customer has adequate assets to address future issues. A decent financial plan can alarm an investor to changes that must be made to guarantee smooth progress through life's economic stages, for example, diminishing spending or changing resource portion. Financial plans ought to likewise be gooey-type, with periodic updates when economic changes happen.

In business, a financial plan can allude to the three essential financial statements (asset report, wage proclamation, and cash flow articulation) made a strategy for success. Financial estimate or financial plan can likewise allude to a yearly projection of pay and costs for an organization, division or office. A financial plan can similarly be an estimation of cash needs and a choice on the best way to raise the cash, for example, through acquiring or issuing additional offers in an organization.

A financial plan may contain prospective financial statements, which are comparative, however different, then a financial plan. Financial arrangements are the ENTIRE financial bookkeeping outline of an organization. Finish financial plans contain all periods and exchange composes. It's a blend of the financial statements which autonomously just mirror a past, present, or future condition of the organization. Financial plans are the accumulation of the verifiable, present, and future financial statements; for instance, a (recorded and display) exorbitant cost from an operational issue is regularly exhibited preceding the issuance of the prospective financial statements which propose an answer for the said operational issue.

The perplexity encompassing the term financial plans may come from the way that there are numerous kinds of fiscal proclamation reports. Separately, financial statements demonstrate either the past, present or future financial outcomes. All the more specifically, financial statements additionally just mirror the specific classes which are pertinent. For example, putting exercises are not sufficiently shown in an asset report. Financial plans are a blend of the individual business statements and mirror all classes of exchanges (tasks and costs and contributing) after some time.

Some period-specific financial articulation cases incorporate pro forma statements (authentic period) and prospective statements (present and future period). Arrangements are a sort of administration which includes "exhibiting, like financial statements, information that is the portrayal of administration." There are two varieties of "prospective financial statements": financial estimates and financial projections and both identify with the present/future day and age. Prospective financial statements are a day and age sort of financial proclamation which may mirror the present/future financial status of an organization utilizing three original reports/financial statements: cash flow articulation, pay explanation, and financial record. "Prospective financial statements are of two sorts gauges and projections. Estimates depend on administration's normal financial position, consequences of activities, and cash flows."

16

Pro Forma statements take beforehand recorded outcomes, the authoritative financial information, and present a "what-if": "what-if" an exchange had happened sooner.

The bookkeeping and fund businesses have particular obligations and parts. At the point when the products of their work are consolidated, it produces an entire picture, a financial plan. A financial examiner thinks about the information and certainties (controls/measures), which are processed, recorded, and exhibited by accountants. Typically, backstaff feels about the info comes about - meaning what has happened or what may happen - and propose an answer for wastefulness. Investors and financial organizations must see both the issue and the solution for settle on an educated choice.

The Financial Plan depicts every one of the exercises, assets, hardware, and materials that are expected to accomplish these goals, and also the time periods included.

The Financial Planning movement includes the accompanying undertakings:

- ❖ Identify the kinds of assets expected to accomplish these targets

- ❖ Affirm the business vision and destinations

- ❖ Quantify the measure of asset (work, hardware, materials)

- ❖ Evaluate the business condition

- ❖ Compute the aggregate cost of each kind of asset

❖ Identify any dangers and issues with the spending set.

❖ Condense the expenses to make a financial plan

Performing Financial Planning is fundamental to the achievement of any association. It provides the Business Plan with thoroughness, by affirming that the destinations set are achievable from a financial perspective. It additionally causes the CEO to set economic focuses for the association, and reward staff for meeting targets inside the spending set.

The part of financial planning incorporates three classifications:

- Key part of financial administration
- Targets of financial administration
- The planning cycle

When drafting a financial plan, the organization ought to set up the planning skyline, which is the time of the method, regardless of whether it be on a here and now (typically a year) or long haul (2– 5 years) premise. Additionally, the individual projects and venture proposals of each operational unit inside the organization ought to be totaled and regarded as one comprehensive project. This practice is known as aggregation.

CHAPTER TWO

UNDERSTANDING THE ELEMENTS OF FINANCIAL PLANNING

To give you the most obvious opportunity for progress, every one of the components beneath is investigated and considered. Some may inquire as to why it's vital to incorporate each region underneath. Think about this relationship: every element of the plan resembles a segment of an ensemble symphony – metal, woodwinds, strings, and percussion. Exclusively, they sound decent. Be that as it may, when played all together, under the direction of an accomplished conductor, who is following the synthesis laid out it turns into a beautiful story. Your exhaustive financial life plan is your creation, written to enable you to accomplish the magnificence of financial freedom.

Cash Flow Planning

Understanding your cash inflows (profit, annuity, and government disability) and cash outflows (everyday costs, income taxes, and savings) is an initial imperative phase of the financial planning process. This report frames the premise from which numerous different reports and examinations are determined, including your retirement cash flow reports.

Retirement Planning

Financial autonomy is a shared objective; regularly characterized as being able to appreciate life and do as you wish without financial concerns. Advances in therapeutic advances and research have brought about individuals living longer; numerous will spend the same number of years resigned as they spent working. While a dynamic and longer life is attractive, it accompanies specific difficulties that should be tended to. Expansion, taxation, and rising therapeutic services costs are a portion of the components that should be considered while deciding how best to accomplish financial autonomy.

Speculation Planning

When building up your speculation technique, there is need to assess your objectives, set aside the opportunity to comprehend your values, consider your chance skyline for required reserves, and perceive your resistance to hazard. Utilizing systems, for example, resource allotment, diversification, and making a bond stepping stool for your cash needs enables us to help diminish risk. The objective of this systematic approach is to lessen vulnerability and also the effect that the unpredictability of the market can have on your portfolio (and your feelings). It likewise expects to provide adaptability and adjust your collection. Venture suggestions are tweaked for every customer.

Insurance Planning

The best of financial plans can come up short if presented to dangers, for example, sudden passing, incapacity, or the requirement for long-haul nursing care. Furthermore, in this inexorably quarrelsome condition, it is fundamental to have adequate individual obligation protection. By assessing and understanding these dangers, we create and actualize a procedure to diminish the conceivably wrecking impacts the startling can have on your financial prosperity.

Income Tax Planning

Proactive tax planning is pivotal to the long haul achievement of your financial and retirement plans. By observing the consistently changing tax laws, we can enable you to use the majority of the open doors that are accessible to you, limiting your tax commitment and augmenting your savings. Procedures may include: tax-productive ventures, gifting, charitable planning, Roth IRA changes, and misfortune (or pick up) collecting.

Education Planning

Putting resources into your kids' or grandchildren's education is speculation that can give back for a lifetime. It opens up incalculable open doors for your beneficiaries, yet with the cost of a school education proceeding to increment, many youthful grown-ups are scrutinizing its esteem. By saving now, even a bit, you can have a major effect in their lives. As a significant aspect of your complete financial life plan, we can enable you to decide an appropriate education financing procedure.

Estate Planning

The reason for estate planning is to guarantee that your desires (by prolonged restorative care, for instance), and also your benefits (who acquires what) are protected when you are never again in charge, either due to ailment or passing. It likewise provides solace to your beneficiaries that they are completing your wants the way you proposed. Our thorough planning approach encourages you to consider your choices and afterward offers practical help to your estate planning lawyer to help draft those records.

CHAPTER THREE

FINANCING STRATEGIES

A financing strategy is essential to an association's vital plan. It sets out how the association plans to back its general tasks to meet its destinations now and later on.

A financing strategy abridges targets, and the moves to be made over a three to five-year time span to accomplish the objectives. It additionally unmistakably states necessary arrangements which will manage those activities.

Quite a lot of cooperation overseas income from various financing and finance sources – from gifts, awards, contracts, and revenue generated from exchanging.

A financial strategy can help you to set objectives and make it less demanding for your board and staff to work towards a more different and stable income blend. It should set out:

- Your current financial circumstance

- What you require financing for

- Your funding targets and how this identity with your central goal

- Your income goes for the following three to five years, including your optimal income blend for the following three to five years, for instance, what level of your income will originate from every income source

- Where you would like to increment or decline revenue

- Your essential financing connections (do you have a substantial association with a specific trust? Is it accurate to say that you are intensely dependent on one contributor?)

- Any new connections that will be basic to accomplishing your targets

- Any assets you have to achieve your financial destinations (individuals, abilities, learning, systems, hardware)

- An investigation of the fundamental dangers and hindrances to financing

- Your store's arrangement: how you will adjust spending and saving.

Your financial strategy ought to be a piece of your general hierarchical strategy or retail strategy.

It ought to be clear how your financial targets line up with your primary goal and broader strategy. Be mindful so as not to pursue financing that will remove distract you from your primary goal.

How does this fit with to your success strategy?

If you need to expand the measure of income you're getting from a specific source; a financial strategy can enable you to distribute appropriate assets to accomplish your financial objectives.

For instance, if you need to build up another giver program, you'll have to guarantee that you have staff or volunteers who can fabricate associations with givers. This can be a significant degree tedious and requires showcasing and relational abilities. It might imply that you won't have the ability to create other financing sources in the meantime. Another giver strategy could influence your plans for enlistment, tasks, promoting and affect detailing, so you'd have to show this inside your retail strategy.

Who ought to be associated with planning for financing and income?

Group funds are something that each staff can get associated with. Similarly, financial planning and strategy isn't something that ought to be restricted to a finance group or the Chief Executing Officer.

Practical financing works when all parts of the association add to the planning and conveyance of a financial strategy.

Keeping in mind the goal to draw in financing, you'll require:

- To be excellent at promoting and showing the effect of what you do to funders, to observing the accomplishment of your exercises

- To have a reasonable thought of how much money you require with a specific end goal to accomplish your targets

- To have a fair vision and a strategy in light of exhaustive information of your arrangement condition and your recipients' needs

- You likewise should be great at overseeing associations with contributors, concede funders, officials or clients.

It's far-fetched that one individual will do these things (in spite of the fact that in some small associations the CEO does a significant portion of them).

Your accountant or CEO can just make projections on the information they're given, so it's imperative that all groups or offices have some familiarity with how they add to the general financial strategy. It can be hard for pledge drives or business advancement directors (i.e., the general population who offer what you do) to take a shot at their own, without the advantage of the bits of knowledge your project staff or interchanges individuals get from conversing with your recipients, accomplices or clients.

Staying up with the latest

Ensure that your success is shared and also remotely, so everybody in your business knows how to promote what you do. It can be useful to have an arrangement of essential details that you share all the time, close by a group pledges objective. This implies the more significant part of your staff have group pledges information readily available, and can in this way be promoting your association constantly.

What is the part of the finance group?

Your finance work – whether that is a group or an individual – can increase the value of both planning and administration. The key parts are:

- Providers of information for primary leadership
- Business administration.

Financial supervisors should survey what information they have, especially expenses and income projections, to have the capacity to control or plan for what's to come. They will likewise provide a precise costing for funders or chiefs. These will demonstrate that you have inquired about any proposed project costs and can make very much educated projections about future turnover and the manageability of the project.

What's the part of the trustee board in planning for financing and income?

The financial administration part of a voluntary association's trustee board is very different to a business association. The three primary financial administration elements of the board are:

Financial view (for instance, guaranteeing that the association's advantages are utilized to seek after its magnanimous destinations)

Procedures (for example, financial controls and hazard administration, distributing yearly reports and records)

Administration (for example, approving annual financial statements and spending plans, guaranteeing appropriate insurances are set up).

Most voluntary associations are financially responsible for a far more prominent number of partners than business associations, which could incorporate the Charity Commission, Companies House, the overall population, neighborhood government and beneficent trusts. The board needs to guarantee that the privilege financial information is gathered and announced inconsistency with the law, and by any agreements or financing understandings.

The entire trustee board must show an incentive for money and viability. They should work with the CEO to guarantee that appropriate checking is set up to demonstrate the effect and sustainability and that assets are being utilized for most extreme esteem.

From the commencement of new business until the point that the point where it turns into a reliably profitable business, all organizations have something in common – the need to finance task and development.

Here are the different ways you may finance another organization:

Bootstrapping

For the most part bootstrapping happens when an organization is subsidized exclusively by the authors without help from outside wellsprings of capital. Doing as such provides organizers with the best measure of adaptability as far as maintaining the business yet also requires the originators to go out on a limb.

Seed Financing

A seed financing regularly includes an unassuming measure of capital contributed to subsidize the examination of a market opportunity or the improvement of the underlying rendition of a product or administration. The originators themselves regularly provide seed financings, "loved ones" or heavenly attendant investors. Commonplace seed financing structures include:

Note Financing: An investor will get an enthusiasm bearing promissory note in return for their speculation, which is either repayable upon request by the investor or upon an expressed development date. A note financing is regularly the least difficult speculation structure and is frequently utilized by originators or "loved ones" investors to enable an organization to keep up its tasks for a brief timeframe before an expected deluge of capital, for example, a Series Seed or Venture Capital Financing or receipt of client income.

Adaptable Note Financing: An investor will get an enthusiasm bearing promissory note in return for their venture, and keep in mind that such bill will incorporate a development date for reimbursement like a conventional note, it will integrate the choice/prerequisite likewise that it be changed over into value (here and there at a marked down rate or subject to some most extreme esteem) at the season of a value financing.

Common Stock Financing: investors get a proprietorship stake in the organization (i.e., they possess a specific level of the organization) as common stock in return for their interest in the organization. This sort of financing can confine capacity to issue common stock choices at low costs.

Series Seed Financing: investors get favored stock in return for their interest in the organization. In addition to other things, investors who hold approved stock regularly get the privilege to recover their venture (in addition to an extra return in a few conditions), called a "favored return," before holders of common stock are paid upon the deal or liquidation of the organization.

Venture Financing

A Venture financing regularly brings about a more significant interest in the organization from at least one investment firms, in return for favored stock of the organization. Notwithstanding getting a favored return like in a Series Seed Financing, Venture investors additionally commonly get vital corporate administration rights, (for example, a seat on the Board of Directors and approval rights on specific exchanges). VC financing regularly happens when an organization can show a significant business chance to rapidly develop the estimation of the organization yet requires considerable capital to do as such.

CHAPTER FOUR

DISTINCTION BETWEEN INVESTMENT MANAGEMENT AND FINANCIAL PLANNING

At the point when an investor enters the market for a financial consultant, it can be challenging to explore the plenty of terms used to depict the kinds of administrations provided.

Financial planning, resource administration, riches administration, speculation administration, portfolio administration, economic life administration, without any end in sight.

Numerous individuals wrongly assume they mean a similar thing. An inability to comprehend the differences between financial administrations and the guides that provide them can make it a test to locate the correct consultant for your specific needs.

WHAT'S THE DIFFERENCE?

There are two central administrations that a consultant offers: financial planning and additionally resource administration (likewise called venture administration and portfolio administration). While they are two separate administrations, they are interrelated and both fundamental to achieving your financial objectives.

Financial planning is a far-reaching evaluation of your financial circumstance and your future objectives. Does it include making a financial plan to enable you to answer vital inquiries, for example, How much do I have to save for retirement? What would it be a good idea for me to do with my 401(k)? How might I support my children's school educations? At the point when would it be advisable for me to petition for Social Security? Does long haul mind insurance bode well?

Resource administration relates to the speculation of your money: constructing your portfolio, building up a proper resource allotment, purchasing and offering securities, rebalancing as required, and so forth.

Adding to the perplexity is the way that financial planning and resource administration firms are both thoughts about venture counselors and must be enrolled accordingly. They may likewise have similar assignments, for example, Certified

Financial Planner or Chartered Financial Analyst. Be that as it may, neither a financial planner nor speculation consultant is required to have any assignments.

A few firms center exclusively on financial planning while others just provide resource administration. Likewise, some financial planners or counselors will straightforwardly deal with financial planning exercises while outsourcing the administration of your money.

Different firms do both. They have a group of financial consultants and their particular in-house venture group who cooperate to provide speculation advice and enable customers to settle on better financial choices.

The rationality is that working with one firm for your financial planning and resource administration needs is more advantageous and practical. It can help guarantee everybody agrees. Rather than juggling numerous individuals and perspectives, you work with a single firm and strategy.

WHAT ARE SERVICES NEEDED?

In the long run, you will probably require both financial planning and resource administration. At the point when and to what degree relies on your age and your riches.

More youthful laborers, by and large, may not require predictable financial planning, as their needs are fundamental – save however much as could reasonably be expected and live underneath your methods.

Be that as it may, as you age and your financial resources develop, things tend to get more convoluted. You need to plan for retirement, purchase another home, save for school, invest more energy in your taxes, decide an appropriate withdrawal rate, make an estate, and so forth.

At last, before you consent to work with any financial professional, do your bit of exploration. Discover what administrations they provide and, similarly as imperative, how they are made up for those administrations.

Most straightforward of all might be to contact the council individually and disclose to them what specific administrations you need. You would prefer not to wind up paying for pretty much then you require.

Costs are descending. It's less expensive than at any other time to exchange. Procedures that were once saved for substantial institutional assets at excessive charges are currently accessible to each investor with minimal effort shared assets and ETFs. The sheer measure of information and registering power available has made everything fair from numerous points of view between the pros and novices entirely. What's more, there is an abundance of speculation books, online journals, investigation, and sentiments from keen, astute individuals if you know where to look.

Sadly, the same cannot be said about financial counsel; A substantial more massive part of what the commercial business calls financial counsel is exceptionally glorified merely product deals.

What's more, as collection administration capacities keep on seeing further innovative picks up later on the rudiments will turn out to be increasingly of an item so that financial advisors will be an enormous differentiator in the financial administration's industry. Anybody can make a portfolio, resource designation or speculation strategy. What a great many people require is exhortation about how their speculations fit into their general financial plan, and all the more vitally their life.

Financial exhortation includes making sense of what well old age has in store for you.

To get the most out of speculation administration, you genuinely need likewise to be accepting great thoroughly considered financial advice. They go as an inseparable unit since you can't make actual blue venture proposals until the point that you comprehend somebody's close to home circumstance.

Ideally, the financial advice business will play get up to speed to venture administration in the years to come.

CHAPTER FIVE

CHOOSING A FINANCIAL PLANNER

Many people think every single financial planner is "certified," however this isn't valid. Anybody can say they are "financial planners." Only a select group of planners who have the certification and recharging requirements of CFP Board can show the CFP® certification marks, which speak to an abnormal state of competency, ethics, and professionalism. CFP Board's Standards of Professional Conduct requires CFP® professionals to put customer interests over their own.

The accompanying five words portray the necessities for getting and keeping up the CFP® certification:

Examination - CFP® professionals must pass the exhaustive two-day CFP® Certification Exam. It tests their capacity to apply financial planning learning to genuine circumstances. The exam covers the financial planning process, tax planning, worker advantages and retirement planning, estate planning, venture administration, what's more, insurance. The regular pass rate for this challenging exam is just 56%.

Enforcement - CFP Board's thorough enactment of her Standards of Professional Conduct, including discharging disciplinary information to people in general, recognizes the CFP® certification from the numerous different assignments in the financial administration's industry. Every individual who looks for CFP® certification is liable to a record verification, and those whose past lead misses the mark regarding CFP Board's ethical and practical measures can be banned from getting to be certified. In the wake of accomplishing certification, a CFP® professional who damages CFP Board's moral and hone norms winds up subject to disciplinary action, up to lasting disavowal of their certification.

Ethics - When it comes to ethics and professional duty, CFP® professionals are held to the most noteworthy of gauges. CFP Board's Code of Ethics plots CFP® professionals' commitments to standards of trustworthiness, objectivity, ability, decency, classification, professionalism, and steadiness. The Rules of Conduct require CFP® professionals to put your interests over their own and to convey their financial planning administrations as a "trustee," acting to the most considerable advantage of their financial planning customers. CFP® professionals are liable to CFP Board sanctions if they disregard these measures.

Experience - Certified Financial Planner™ professionals must have at least of 3 years experience in financial planning preceding procuring the privilege to make use of the CFP® certification marks.

Education - CFP® professionals must build up their open and functional financial planning learning by finishing a far-reaching course of study at a school or college that offers a financial planning educational modules approved by CFP Board. CFP® professionals are required to finish 30 hours of proceeding with education (CE) like clockwork. This incorporates 2 hours of CFP Board approved Ethics CE. CFP Board must process all revealed CE hours at the very latest the termination date with a specific end goal to keep away from certification lapse.

What to look for;

Try to check the accompanying when you think about a financial counselor or planner:

- They should know your conditions including your venture destinations, speculation skyline, learning and experience (counting any information of subordinates), financial circumstance and hazard resilience (counting danger of loss of capital), and painstakingly assess your hazard profile before making any methodologies or financial product proposals to you.

- They should give you proper explanations of why prescribed products are reasonable for you and the nature and degree of dangers the speculation products bear. They ought to likewise report and provide you with a duplicate of the method of reasoning basic the speculation proposals made to you.

- In delivering administrations including ancillary products, they should guarantee that you comprehend the nature and dangers of suggested products and that you have sufficient total assets to have the capacity to accept the risks and bear the potential misfortunes of exchanging the products.

CONCLUSION

Thank you once again for downloading this book!

When we understand the financial statements of a firm, and we have to conjecture them; we can discover a few circumstances, yet specifically we can discover two unique situations: it is possible that we have recorded information on costs and volumes per product or benefit and apparently, the deals incomes from the financial statements or we just have the information from the financial assertion, to be specific deals incomes, expenses, and costs.

Besides, it may be difficult to assess the time spent in each occasion of administration. For this situation, some additional knowledge could advise the examiner to investigate the firm movement as far as the number of administration occasions adjusted in the year. This may be less demanding to identify and could illuminate the expert in the evaluating of the administration.

Finally, if you enjoyed this book, then I will like to ask you for a favor, would you be kind enough to leave a review for this book? It will be greatly appreciated

Thank You and Goodluck